MW00620697

Namarupa:
The Magic
of Tantra Mantra

by

Phillip Hurley & Leigh Hurley

Maithuna Publications

2012

Namarupa: The Magic of Tantra Mantra

Copyright ©2012 by Phillip Hurley and Leigh Hurley

Illustrations ©2012 by Leigh Hurley

Series: The Sadhaka's Guide, Volume 2

Notice of Rights

All rights reserved. No part of this book may be reproduced or transmitted in any form or by any means, electronic, mechanical, photocopying, recording or otherwise without prior written permission of the publisher. To request permission to use any parts of this book, please contact Good Idea Creative Services, permission@goodideacreative.com.

Maithuna Publications is an imprint of:
Good Idea Creative Services
324 Minister Hill Road
Wheelock VT 05851 USA

ISBN 978-0-9837847-4-6

Library of Congress Control Number: 9780983784746

Library of Congress subject headings:
Mantras--Handbooks, manuals, etc.
Tantrism--Handbooks, manuals, etc.
Sanskrit language--Terms and phrases
Kundalini--Handbooks, manuals, etc.

Authors' website:

www.tantrayoga.us

Contents

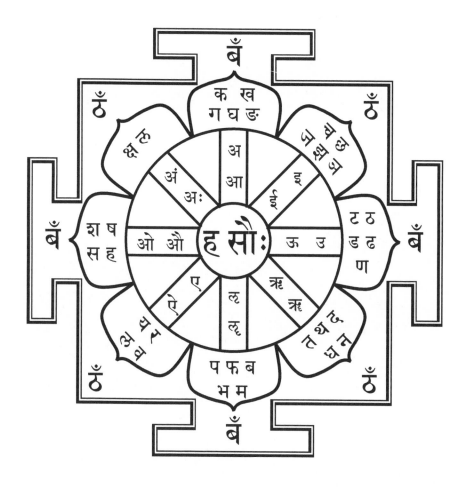

मातृका यन्त्र

Mātṛkā Yantra

Mandala of the Sanskrit alphabet

Foreword

I began my study and practice of mantra in the latter part of the 1960s, an exciting time to search for and learn new things. I was not interested in the drug-induced changes of consciousness that were popular at the time. I preferred and kept to a more natural transformation that meditation and mantra provided.

I was also interested in magic - real magic! I loved the idea of Aladdin's lamp, genii, flying carpets, and so on. But this was a path not well-trodden, with few reliable maps or sign-posts to guide.

At this time I was initiated by a swami and given my first lessons in the powers of mantra. However, I found that once the portal was opened for me, I was essentially on my own to further discover and explore. Although my attempts were somewhat sporadic, my strong interest was consistent, and I put in enough effort to move ever deeper into realms that most people would find astounding. I found my magic carpet in the form of astral projection. I could leave my body and literally fly through the air as well as visit other dimensions of time and space. I have experienced the materialization and de-materialization of matter, and have discovered that genii are very real, or at last as real as we are.

While this probably sounds preposterous to many readers, those are the facts based on my own experience. I invite you to experiment and experience the effects of this ancient art in your own life by chanting mantra.

Phillip Hurley

Namarupa ~ Name and Form

What is mantra?

In Sanskrit the word mantra means "instrument of the mind." It is a magical tool that brings us to understand and master manifest form, and also leads us to moksha (liberation/enlightenment).

Mantra is sound, vibration and thus movement. In Sanskrit, this movement is called *spanda, vak, shabda,* or *nada,* depending upon which level of movement you are referring to. Simply explained:

Vak relates to the sound and vibrations of speech.

Spanda is the vibration/movement of subtle energies as they coalesce into form from formlessness.

Nada is the essence of sound.

Shabda is the manifestation of nada in the physical and non-physical worlds.

The total process of movement, the sound of the universe, is expressed in the mantra *Oṁ (or Auṁ)* ॐ whose three letters represent the creation, preservation and dissolution of manifest form.

Mantra brings us to a quantum-level awareness of the universal creative matrix of which we are a part. When practicing mantra, you intentionally affect the nature of reality and thus change what is around you and within you. Mantra always affects manifestation/reality, however, the degree to which this occurs depends on your level of practice, discipline and understanding.

Mantra has potent effects on the physical, emotional and mental components of our being. It can clear the subconscious mind of unwanted samskaras, the tendencies and patterns from our past (this life and others) that interfere with our movement towards moksha/liberation. The sound of each mantra transmutes and transforms us and our environment in accord with the nature of the mantra.

It is important to understand that mantra is kundalini! Meditate on this fact every time you begin a mantra. Everything in existence is a manifestation of kundalini, and mantra is directly connected to kundalini energy. Mantra is the language of kundalini, the user interface, if you will.

Tantric cosmology

According to Tantric cosmology, the universe in all its dimensions resides within Brahman. Brahman has two major attributes. One attribute is Brahman without form, *nirguna*. The other is Brahman with form, *saguna*. Saguna Brahman comes into being through Brahman's creative self, called Brahma. Brahma can be understood as the tao, represented by the yin and yang symbol.

The phenomenal world within the tao is created, sustained and dissolved through the inter-action of Shiva/yang and Shakti/yin. Shiva represents the Sun, yang, male principle, the elements fire and air, and electricity. Shakti represents the Moon, yin, female principle, water and earth elements, and magnetism. In Tantra the whole of this inter-active process (create - sustain - dissolve) is represented by the goddess Kali.

The necklace of Kali

Kali is adorned with a necklace, known as *varnamala* or "garland of letters." Each bead represents an *akshara* (letter) of the Devanagari alphabet and thus a particular vibration and primal form. The necklace is often depicted with a skull for each letter or bead. The skulls remind us of the hidden structure behind form, and that form is impermanent. Every interaction between Shiva and Shakti manifests the Kali principle, which is movement through time and space.

This movement of desire through space and time is represented by the *kama kala* triangle. This symbol is often used in the *janana* ritual, which is the ritual of giving birth to, of the mantra's coming into existence. In janana ritual, the mantra is placed at the center of a triangle, the yoni from which the mantra comes forth. Kama kala is the desire between Shiva and Shakti and the *lila* (sport, play) between them, which produce movement in space and thus time.

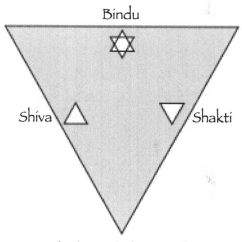

The kama-kala triangle

Kali is the goddess of time, which in western mythology is commonly represented by Father Time and the planet Saturn. Saturn also represents all the forms of manifestation. Each form has a particular name or vibration rate, and hence, mantra. This relationship and the study of it is called *namarupa*, "name and form." Every form has a name, sound, vibratory rate, and every name, sound and vibratory rate has a form.

Another word for form is *artha* which means material and/or object when talking about physical form. Mantra nama calls into being its respective form, or mantra rupa. Each form also evokes and calls into being a certain sound/ vibration/feeling nama. Thus physical objects such as flowers, statues, incense, colors, garments, music and so forth are used in *puja* (ritual of reverence) to evoke a particular vibratory rate.

Each letter or combination of letters on the necklace of Kali creates a vibration that calls into being a certain form, and each form evokes certain mantras.

A mantra is form and or sound according to your understanding and has mystical and magical effects.

The Practice of Mantra

Mantra, like anything else, requires work and dedication. The process of *japa* (constantly repeating a mantra) can at times feel tedious, but remember that you are working through your karma with the practice of mantra siddhi yoga.

For the most part you should find the practice of mantra to be an enjoyable process. Benefits, however subtle, can be noticed from the very start of practice. If performed daily, you will experience an eventual transformation of your life that feels good and brings good fortune to you.

Be practical and down to earth when considering mantra, and patient. The fruits of mantric practice take time to ripen. For most of us, many changes have to occur in the physical, emotional and mental spheres of our being in order for us to be able to consciously realign our selves in relation to cosmic forces. Such conscious alignment is fundamentally what the practice of yoga consists of. Mantra as a tool brings about the changes necessary for us to become a template that shapes cosmic energies more according to our intent, instead of us being a puppet to our samskaras and karma.

It is very much like the disciplines of tai chi or martial arts in which the physical body is trained, and capabilities are built up over time. Just like our physical bodies, our minds and emotional selves also require a sequence of training and growth. Be patient and consistent. For the most part, enlightenment comes in increments.

Balance

Your practice of mantra will be enhanced if you try to live a balanced lifestyle. Be thoughtful about what you do.

Be moderate in eating, drinking and other activities. Unhealthy food and excessive amounts of any food should be avoided. A few simple hatha yoga postures practiced on a daily basis can be very helpful. A mild physical, emotional, and mental asceticism should be practiced in order to create and maintain more balance of your ida and pingala channels, which are the solar and lunar currents in your body, often referred to as yin and yang.

Reasons for doing mantra

Classically there are six uses for mantra:

ॐ *Shanti* - to obtain *moksha* (liberation), calmness of mind, prosperity, healing, learning and wisdom.

ॐ *Vasikarana* - to attract and influence people or circumstances, and tame forces to maintain order. It is like gardening in that you choose plants to grow and weed out others so that your intended crop can grow to fruition.

ॐ *Stambhana* - to stop and restrain those who wish to harm you and keep you from moksha.

ॐ *Vidvesana* - to create aversion, between people, organizations and allies that wish to harm you and keep you from moksha.

ॐ *Ucchatana* - to overthrow, and upset those who wish to harm you or keep you from moksha and cause them to quit.

ॐ *Marana* - to destroy those who wish to harm you or keep you from moksha.

The karmic benefits and consequences of the use of mantras depend upon circumstances of application, the particular mantra and who is applying the mantra.

Certain of these groups of mantras can be aimed at our own inner problems as well as outer circumstance.

We speak of the classical purposes of mantra, but this is not endorsement of their use in a negative manner. A mantra is simply a tool, like a knife. A knife can be used to slice vegetables, or to inflict bodily harm for no reason. In the practice of mantra, you will discover, sooner or later, that it is not in your best interest to harm or interfere with others unless necessary. However, the word "necessary," is rather vague and depends on the karmic understanding of the user of the word. A possible example of necessity would be Sri Aurobindo's well-documented occult intervention during World War II to stop the Axis powers from gaining an upper hand.

A person of lesser understanding would likely not completely grasp the karmic trajectories of some outcome they might truly believe to be "necessary."

Tantrics jokingly say that the best way to stop your enemies from harming you is to chant mantras for their enlightenment. It is a bit like showing a cross to a vampire - they will want to run away. Of course, if that doesn't work, the Tantric will tell you to chant mantra for your own enlightenment because you will need it.

Despite all the above, the main purpose of mantra is to gain knowledge and experience of the cosmos; and thus, enlightenment.

Enlivening mantra

It is often said that a guru is necessary to enliven the power of a mantra for a student. This is true, but what is not said is that the guru resides within you, in your thousand petaled lotus.

If a guru embodied in human form manifests on the physical plane and gives you *diksha* (giving of mantra or initiation), it is simply because your inner guru has given this individual the privilege to act on its behalf. A physically embodied guru is not necessary for diksha. The wisdom and knowledge we seek is already present within us. External events are nothing but projected symbols of our inner processes of transformation. We are each literally walking within our own minds.

Traditionally it is stated that various elements need to be present for a mantra to become efficacious. Practices vary from tradition to tradition. Some are quite strict with many rules and others are lenient with few rules.

When you select a mantra or it is given to you, try to understand or learn what it means, and learn how to pronounce it correctly. In some cases you will not initially understand the meaning of the mantra, but through practice (japa) the meaning will be revealed to you. For one reason or another, you may not know exactly how to pronounce the mantra correctly. Do not be overly concerned about this. Sincerity, effort and faith will reward you with the siddhi of the mantra despite any error.

Much depends on the state of understanding of the *sadhaka* (magician) as to what is needed for the correct performance of mantra.

To illustrate I offer this story:

Once upon a time there was a monk who, after many years of hard work and meditation, was privileged to be elected to head the monastery he lived in. He was proud of his position, and rightly so for he had helped many people on the path to enlightenment, in accord with his order's teachings. But, being human, as time went on, he put on the cloak and demeanor of a superior being and even thought himself a bodhisattva of sorts. He went to power lunches, had a cellphone and drove an expensive car, as befitted his station in life.

It came to pass that he heard of a hermit who lived in a cave across a small lake not too far from the monastery, who was purported to cause miracles whenever he came across the lake and into the town begging for food. The monk concluded that this hermit must be a trickster as he had never attended a monastery, and the monk plotted to expose the hermit. The monk put on a disguise, left his car in the monastery garage and set out to town to await the hermit's routine visit. He finally reached town and not being accustomed to walking such distances, his feet hurt quite a bit; so, he went to the shore of the lake near the town. As he refreshed his feet in the cool water of the lake he saw the reflection of a man appear on the water above his own reflection. It startled him.

He turned around quickly and was greeted by a swift "Hello," and a smile, "been here long?"

"No," said the monk, "I just got here and am waiting for the hermit who lives across the lake to come by. They say he performs miracles by his very presence, but I'm sure it's just folderol fakery. Such chicanery hurts the image of the monks who spend many long years of discipline, chanting the most sacred and secret mantras. This person is no doubt a simpleton and a charlatan."

"Yes, the neighborhood is deteriorating," said the man. "Charlatans everywhere. Mind if I sit here for a while and chant while I wait for the lake to become more calm so that I can cross safely?"

The monk delighted to hear that the man wanted to chant. "Let's chant together," he said.

The man started chanting. As he chanted, the monk's face twisted into a grimace at what he was hearing.

"I can't take this any more" said the monk "your pronunciation is all wrong. You will never gain siddhis chanting like that."

"Really," said the man, "do you mean I have been doing it wrong all these years?"

"Yes," said the monk. "Pay attention and I will teach you the proper pronunciation," whereupon the monk chanted the mantra correctly.

"I am so grateful," said the man. "All these years I have practiced this mantra, and now I am ashamed that I have wasted so much time. I should have come to the monastery to learn the proper pronunciation. Well, at least I have it now, thank you."

The man stood up and said, "It looks like the lake is calm enough to cross now."

The monk looked puzzled for a second and said, "Where is your boat?"

As the words slipped from the monk's mouth, the man began walking across the surface of the lake toward the opposite shore. He turned around to answer the monk and said, "I don't need a boat if the waters are calm but when it is rough a boat helps. Thank you for the mantra."

The monk was speechless and struck immobile as he saw the hermit become smaller and smaller and disappear out of sight. He went back to the monastery that night, gave his cell phone and car to the most ambitious monk he could find, left the monastery and was never heard of again.

The most profound experiences can come from unorthodox sources. All scriptures, traditions, teachers, gurus and priests fall down before that faith and devotion which can move mountains.

That said, here are the basic elements of classical mantra practice:

Basic elements of classical mantra practice

꠹ *Mantroddhara* - selection of a mantra, usually from a sacred text or magical formula. But, you may also be given a mantra in a dream, or by a guru or a friend; and there are families that pass down mantras from generation to generation, kept secret from outsiders. I have witnessed the potency of such a mantra, used by member of a Brahmin family who had no training in mantra practice, other than being given this mantra. The effects were quite extraordinary.

꠹ *Purascharana* - the rite of preparation or introduction. In mantra siddhi yoga this term generally has come to mean the number of repetitions of the mantra needed in order to attain the *siddha* (magical power) of the mantra.

꠹ *Chaitanya* - infusing the mantra with universal soul or spirit, consciousness, intelligence.

꠹ *Sadhana* - the type of mantra practice, such as *likhita* japa.

꠹ *Samskara* - the performance of ten rituals to remove any blemish from the mantra or any blockage of your ability to access the power of the mantra. Samskaras are karmic tendencies from the past that influence current actions.

The ten rituals to remove samskaras

꠹ *Dipana* - kindling - lighting a lamp or candle. This can be an external ritual, or simply visualized.

꠹ *Janana* - giving birth to the mantra. This is in fact already accomplished when you become aware of a mantra. However, there are many rituals that develop this theme. One such ritual is to draw a kama-kala triangle representing the yoni, write the mantra into the triangle, and recite the mantra 108 times or more prefixing it with

Oṁ Hrīṁ Śrīṁ Klīṁ

ॐ ह्रीँ श्रीँ कलीँ

and suffixing it with

Oṁ Klīṁ Śrīṁ Hrīṁ

ॐ कलीँ श्रीँ ह्रीँ

ॐ *Bodhana* - discovery of what the mantra means. You may or may not initially understand the full meaning of a specific mantra, but through practice you will be enlightened as to its full meaning. The mantra can be prefixed and suffixed with the mantra

Hrūṁ

हूँ

which gives understanding of the inner meaning of the mantra.

ॐ *Abhisheka* - ritual bathing, performed by writing the mantra on a palm leaf and then pouring water from the river Ganges upon it. Of course, if Ganges river water is not available, any water will do that is spiritually considered to be Ganges water. While pouring the water over the palm leaf, the mantra

Aiṁ Haṁsa Oṁ

ऐं हंस ओं

is repeated 108 times.

ॐ *Vimalikarana* - preparation of the mantra for infusion of life force. This is accomplished by prefixing and suffixing the chosen mantra with the mantra

Oṁ Troṁ Vaṣat

ॐ त्रों वषट्

and repeated 108 times.

ॐ *Jivana* - infusion of life force into the mantra is accomplished by prefixing and suffixing the mantra with

Svadhā Vaṣat
स्वधा वषट्

repeated 108 times.

ॐ *Tadana* - activation of the protective and striking power of the mantra. Each mantra has a protective nature and a weapon (astra) associated with it. This power is brought to the fore by pronouncing the mantra 108 times while prefixing and suffixing it with the mantra

Phaṭ
फट्

ॐ *Gopana* - guarding, protecting and preserving the mantra. This is often accomplished by prefixing and suffixing the bija

Hrīṁ
ह्रीँ

108 times to the mantra you wish to protect. This mantra forms a shield that keeps away negative psychic forces and maintains the integrety of the mantra.

ॐ *Tarpana* - worship by ritual offering, usually water, milk, ghee, curd or honey. The mantra is written upon a palm leaf and bathed with these substances. The mantra soaks up the prana of the substances and is thus given physical nourishment to perform physical effects.

ॐ *Apyayana* - causing the mantra to thrive and come to a complete fullness. This is accomplished by reciting the mantra daily.

This is the short list. Depending upon what treatise you read, this list could be extended to hundreds of observances and rituals that surround the recitation of mantra.

Ritual provides excellent support for consciousness. It is important because we are bombarded daily with a variety of efforts to engage our energies to serve the purposes of others. With ritual we reclaim our energies and focus them in the direction we wish to go.

We present here an updated understanding and a simplified form of practice that is short, to the point, and effective. Most of our students have been satisfied with these techniques; and of course you can always add any of the previously mentioned ritual details as you feel you need to, in accord with your karma. Know that you can be creative in your mantra practice, and be free to add what delights you and makes the practice meaningful for you.

Initiation of a mantra

The *sahasrara*, also known as the thousand petal lotus, is located above your head and has within it the guru chakra. The guru chakra is your guru, your "higher self."

A good way to begin your relationship with any new mantra is to transfer your consciousness to your guru chakra in your thousand petaled lotus, and chant the mantra 108 times.

Alternatively, you can transfer your consciousness into your sahasrara, then transfer yourself along with your sahasrara into the center of the circle (the bindu point) of the guru chakra mandala. First chant the Guru/Saraswati mantra 108 times,

Aiṁ

followed by chanting the mantra you want to enliven 108 times.

Then, leave the mantra in the thousand petaled lotus, or in the bindu circle of the guru chakra yantra. Leave it there for 24 to 48 hours.

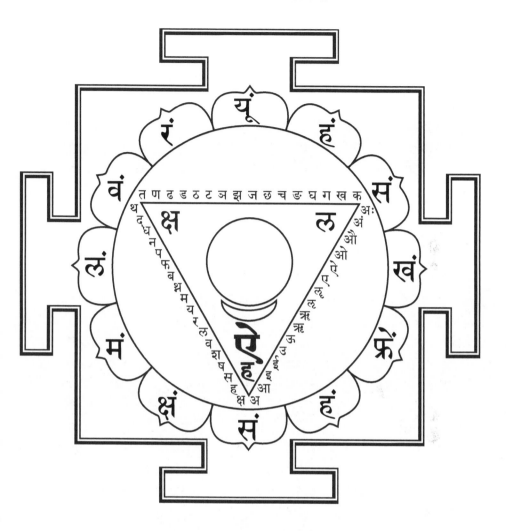

Guru chakra yantra

When you return to the sahasrara, thank the guru for giving you the mantra and infusing it with power and blessings.

Your sahasrara contains within it all the powers and qualities of manifest existence.

When placed in the sahasrara the mantra is infused with energy and becomes alive. For each person the results of this diksha will depend upon what your inner guru allows.

Japa

Japa is the repetitive chanting of a mantra. Most mantra manuals state that a certain number of repetitions (usually many thousand) are necessary for the mantra to become fully activated. The numbers are not so much exact magic formulas, as they are guides for how much practice is needed to install the thought patterns in our mental, astral, and physical bodies.

When you think, feel, speak or move you are using prana, and giving it form, whether thought, feeling, sound, or physical movement. Most people's thoughts and feelings are ruled by their samskaras, unconscious set-in patterns from the past; so, the form they give to prana is also shaped by their samskaras. Mantra is intended to replace the prana templates created by our samskaras with new templates of our choosing. With sufficient repetition, the thought form of a mantra is set in and solidifies, and becomes a template to filter raw undefined energies and give them shape. In alchemy this process is referred to as "fixing the volatile."

Whether we realize it or not, mantras do work immediately, but the full strength may not be felt initially. The whole effectiveness of a mantra will manifest over time.

It is not strictly necessary to count the repetitions of mantra - if you keep at it, sooner or later you will reach the number of repetitions necessary and the mantra will be enlivened. Note that, according to your karma, a mantra may work on the first repetition, or 100,000 repetitions later.

Still, the use of a mala to keep track of repetitions is an engaging ritual and therefore a very powerful tool. Mala means "string of beads" in Sanskrit. A typical mala has 108

Rudraksha mala

beads with the addition of a bindu or meru bead for a total of 109 beads. 108 is a sacred number and is a base for the number of repetitions.

To use a mala in a traditional manner, drape the beads over the middle finger of the right hand. Grasp the bead just after the meru bead between your thumb and middle finger, and then move one bead forward with your thumb for each repetition of the mantra until you come to the 108th bead, next to the bindu/meru bead.

The bindu/meru bead marks the beginning and end of the mala, and is never crossed during japa. For more than 108 repetitions, instead of crossing the meru bead, turn the beads around and go back in the direction from which you came.

Holding the mala

Malas can be made from any type of bead, but the most common have either rudraksha or sandlewood beads. Rudraksha is related to Shiva/yang and thus the beads are considered "hot." They are male, electric, energizing and exceptionally good to bring in healing prana to the physical body. Sandlewood is related to Shakti/yin, and so is more of a soothing, magnetic vibration than rudraksha. It also is healing but in a different way.

Some people find the rudraksha too energizing and prefer to use sandlewood beads. Others find the fire of rudraksha to be just the type of energy needed. You can also use tulsi (sacred basil), gold, silver, or copper beads, gem stones for different planets, and so on. You can use one mala for all of your mantra japa, or a different mala for each mantra, or anything in between.

Malas can be kept in your puja space after use, or worn. Wearing a mala surrounds you with the vibration of the mantra chanted with the mala.

Another item sometimes worn to facilitate mantra practice is parad, which is fixed mercury, usually worn as a ring or a bead. Mercury, also known as quicksilver, is a liquid metal. The mercury is solidified and rendered non-toxic through ayurvedic alchemical operations.

The truth of the claim that parad is non-toxic has not been proven to the satisfaction of various government agencies. For this reason we must caution the reader, and for the sake of public record, state that, according to the current view of the medical establishment on the matter, you should not work with it. We do

Parad ring

work with it and have found wearing parad to be a potent adjunct to mantra practice.

Parad has an affinity with the akasha mantra and the akasha (Mercury) chakra at the back of the neck. This chakra relates to sound, speech and mantra, and the power of the word. Parad balances the solar and lunar forces, which allows the consciousness to enter *sushumna* with greater ease when raising kundalini.

In the Western pantheon, Mercury is the the messenger of the gods. The caduceus of Mercury represents the spinal chakra system, with the ida and pingala channels represented by two serpents. In astrology, the planet Mercury rules communication and the metal mercury.

Modes of Chanting

According to Tantra yoga we have more than one body. We have a physical body and a number of other subtle bodies, or sheaths, called *koshas*. Each kosha inhabits and relates to different *lokas* (worlds, or planes of existence). The three most important lokas are in the West referred to as the physical world, astral world, and the mental world.

Performing a mantra in a certain manner is said to affect some planes of existence and subtle bodies more than others.

ॐ *Uccaih japa* - Mantra spoken aloud affects the physical body and physical surroundings strongly.

ॐ *Upamshu japa* - Mantra spoken in a whisper or very low voice strongly affects the etheric astral plane, and thus the feelings and emotions.

ॐ *Manasika japa* - Mantra spoken in the mind/spirit affects the mind, mental body, and mental plane directly.

Of course mantra chanted in any fashion will affect the total self; but if you have an application specifically aimed at the mind, emotional body, or physical body, you can target the mantra with one of the three modes.

A sequence of the modes can be used to bring a mantra down through the subtler lokas into physical being with more clarity and quickness. In other words, chant the mantra mentally/silently, then in a whisper, and then aloud. Conversely, to dissolve a certain trait or bring your consciousness to a more refined state, reverse the sequence and chant physically first, then whisper and then silently.

Ideally, when chanting mantra, face east during the day and north at night. The best times of day to practice are sunrise, noon, sunset and midnight (see page 109 for more detail); but any time and facing any direction will suffice.

One can sit in a chair or on the floor, with or without cushions or back support; or lie down on a bed, floor, or couch if you like. If you are familiar with hatha yoga, padmasana, swastikasana, or siddhasana are good asanas for mantra; or simply cross your legs comfortably while sitting on the floor. What is most important is to be comfortable. If you are not comfortable, you will not enjoy or benefit as much from the practice.

Mantra can also be performed while you are engaged in physical activity. It can be integrated into the rhythms of your movement and breathing when walking, running or any other repetitive physical activities, whether household chores or an exercise routine.

Pranayama and Mantra

Coupling your breath cycle with chanting is a potent method for realizing mantras, but it is not necessary to use specific pranayama (breathing) techniques for chanting mantra. As you learn a particular mantra, you will find a comfortable breath cycle for it. Details are offered here only for the sake of completeness and so that you may be aware of further options for your practice.

Kumbhaka

Between ingoing and outgoing breaths resides a state in which any mantra has great efficacy. It is a balance point known as bindu, akasha, and/or sushumna, in which the alternating breath polarity (inhale/exhale, Shakti/Shiva, yin/yang) stops, and the two polarities become one and cease to exist individually. The practice of stopping the breath is called *kumbakha*. It is the conjunction of the Sun and Moon and the negation of time and space.

Kumbhaka is generally classified as either *sahit* and *kevala*.

In sahit kumbhaka, the breath is gradually slowed down to temporarily cease breath. Certain pranayama (breathing exercises) lead to a natural, voluntary, temporary breath suspension.

ॐ *Antar kumbhaka* is the suspension of breath when inhalation (poorak) is complete.

ॐ *Bahya kumbhaka* is the suspension of breath when exhalation (rechak) is complete.

Kevala kumbhaka is the voluntary cessation of breath outside of the context of performing pranayama exercises; however, it is usually a result of the ongoing daily practice of sahit. In kevala you do not feel a need for an in-breath or out-breath and are totally relaxed and at ease. It feels natural and is not a forced holding of the breath.

Sanskrit Quick Reference and Pronunciation Guide

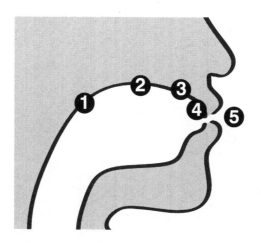

The illustration shows the mouth positions and parts of tongue used to contact them for correct pronunciation of Sanskrit letters.

1. *Guttural.* Back part of tongue is used.
2. *Palatal.* Top part of tongue used.
3. *Cerebral.* Tip of the tongue is used.
4. *Dental* (behind teeth). Tip of the tongue is used
5. *Labial* (at the lips). Tongue is not used

All of the consonants in the alphabet are followed by an "a" sound as in the word another.

Sanskrit Letter Tables

Vowels, anusvara and visarga

Sanskrit	Abrev.	Translit	Sounds like	As in
अ		a	a	another
आ	ा	ā	a	father
इ	ि	i	i	pin
ई	ी	ī	ee	beet
उ	ु	u	u	push
ऊ	ू	ū	oo	mood
ऋ	ृ	ṛ	r	acre
ॠ	ॄ	ṝ	r	acre but longer
ऌ	ॢ	ḷ	l	table
ॡ	ॣ	ḹ	l	table but longer
ए	े	e	e	cafe
ऐ	ै	ai	ai	aisle
ओ	ो	o	o	yoke
औ	ौ	au	ow	flout
अं	ं	aṁ	nasal m	(anusvara)
अः	ः	aḥ	soft ha sound	(visarga)

Semi-vowels

Sanskrit	Translit	Sounds like	As in	Sanskrit	Translit	Sounds like	As in
य	ya	y	yes	ल	la	l	love
र	ra	r	run	व	va	v	vine

Consonants

SAN-SKRIT	TRANS-LIT	SOUNDS LIKE	AS IN	SAN-SKRIT	TRANS-LIT	SOUNDS LIKE	AS IN
क	ka	k	kite	ढ	ḍha	dh	red hot
ख	kha	kh	Eckhart	ण	ṇa	n	horn
ग	ga	g	go	त	ta	t	stop
घ	gha	gha	dig hard	थ	tha	th	hot house
ङ	ṅa	n	sing	द	da	d	dose
च	ca	ch	chair	ध	dha	dh	adhoc
छ	cha	chh	staunch heart	न	na	n	nap
ज	ja	j	jam	प	pa	p	pot
झ	jha	jh	hedge-hog	फ	pha	ph	up hill
ञ	ña	ny	canyon	ब	ba	b	bat
ट	ṭa	t	tub	भ	bha	bh	rub hard
ठ	ṭha	th	light house	म	ma	m	moon
ड	ḍa	d	dove				

Sibilants

SAN-SKRIT	TRANS-LIT	SOUNDS LIKE	AS IN
श	śa	sh	ship
ष	ṣa	sh	shine
स	sa	s	sun

Aspirant

SAN-SKRIT	TRANS-LIT	SOUNDS LIKE	AS IN
ह	ha	h	home

Special Letter

SAN-SKRIT	TRANS-LIT	SOUNDS LIKE	AS IN
क्ष	kṣa	ksh	action

gutteral	dental
labial	palatal
cerebral	

Sanskrit Letter Portraits and Meanings

The meaning of the letters

Each Sanskrit letter is a mantra. We have listed some meanings for the letters but the reader should be cautioned to meditate on each letter and discover for themselves the deeper meanings. Entire books could be written about each letter just to explain the letter's nature and effects.

The figure in the lower left corner of each page shows the order of pen or brush strokes for writing the letter.

Anusvara

Chanting letters as mantras can be done with or without the addition of *anusvara* (nasal m sound).

Nada bindu or *chandra bindu* is the point at which sound emerges from akasha and is of great importance. It is represented by the anusvara - a dot ˙ above the letter - or, as chandra bindu - a dot and crescent ˘ above the letter. At the physical level it is intoned at the bridge of the nose and slides down to the closed lips as an "mmm" sound; or, can be intoned at the bridge of the nose without sliding down to the lips; or simply intoned with the lips.

Chanted aloud in full voice, this sound vibrates the physical body - cells, organs, glands. Whispered it works upon the etheric/astral body, and when silently intoned it affects the mind.

For the most part, to discover, understand, and experience the essence of the letter, the anusvara is added to the letter in meditation.

a (a) as in ***another.***

Wisdom, knowledge, health and
longevity, protection, pure existence.

Calligraphy

ā (a) as in *father.*

Creates attraction and affection and enhances speech, bliss, awareness, contentment, creativity.

Abbreviation T

Calligraphy

i (*i*) as in *pin.*

Use of spiritual realization, wisdom and
knowledge, and giving it direction, focus.
Promotes a healthy body and general well-being.

Abbreviation

Calligraphy

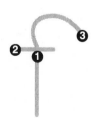

ī *(ee)* as in **beet.**

Purifies, and gives excellent
speaking abilities.

Abbreviation

Calligraphy

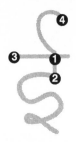

u (u) as in *push.*

Penetrating and permeating everything. Vitality and strength.

Abbreviation

Calligraphy

ū (oo) as in ***mood***.

Spiritual strength, penetrates and
permeates everything.
Time and space.

Abbreviation

Calligraphy

ṛ (r) as in *acre.*

Agitates, stirs to action.

Abbreviation

Calligraphy

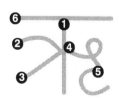

ṝ (r) as in *acre* but longer.

Creates splendor and charm.

Abbreviation

Calligraphy

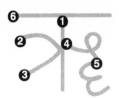

ḷ (l) as in ***table.***

Causes confusion and puzzlement for the logical mind,
but sets the stage for meditation.

Calligraphy

Ḹ (ḷ) as in *table* but longer.

Causes confusion and puzzlement for the logical mind
but sets the stage for meditation.

Calligraphy

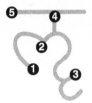

e (e) as in *cafe.*

Creates charm, feeling and sensation.

Abbreviation

Calligraphy

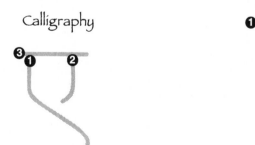

ai (ai) as in *aisle.*

Opens the way to wisdom and knowledge.
Creates charm, feeling and sensation.

Abbreviation

Calligraphy

o (o) as in *yoke.*

Rising above lower consciousness.
Clarifies speech and consciousness.

Abbreviation

Calligraphy

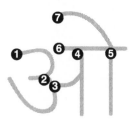

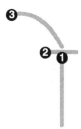

au (ow) as in *flout.*

Creates a platform for your presentations. Has the power of subjugation.

Abbreviation

Calligraphy

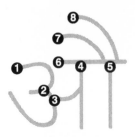

aṁ (nasal *m*)

Spiritual balance, realization. Said to give control over animals and less evolved instinctually controlled humans. Causes confusion.

Abbreviation

Calligraphy

aḥ (soft *ha* sound)

Said to promote longevity and is
powerful in nature.

Abbreviation **:**

Calligraphy

ka (k) as in *kite.*

Power, omnipotence, happiness,
prosperity.

Calligraphy

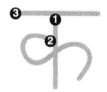

47

kha (kh) as in *Eckhart.*

Causes agitation. Good for
rearranging events, ideas and feelings .

Calligraphy

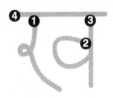

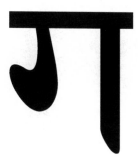

ga (g) as in *go.*

Wealth, remover of obstacles.

Calligraphy

gha (gha) as in *dig hard.*

Remover of subtle obstacles, stops things that are not good for you and gives good fortune.

Calligraphy

ṅa (n) as in *sing.*

Is mighty.

Calligraphy

ca (ch) as in *chair.*

Can be used to remove obstacles.

Calligraphy

cha (chh) as in **staunch-heart.**

Is formidable.

Calligraphy

ja (j) as in *jam.*

Nurturing, sexual attraction,
destroys evil and fear.

Calligraphy

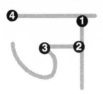

jha (jh) as in *hedgehog.*

Removes an unspiritual attitude.

Calligraphy

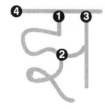

ña (ny) as in *canyon.*

Gives longevity.

Calligraphy

ṭa (ṭ) as in *tub.*

Penetrating, nails things down, and can pierce.

Calligraphy

ṭha (th) as in *light-house.*

Gives pleasure and
aids concentration.

Calligraphy

ḍa (ḍ) as in *dove.*

A powerful sound that
gives protection.

Calligraphy

ḍha (dh) as in *red-hot.*

Gives wealth.

Calligraphy

ṇa (n) as in *horn.*

Gives success and causes infatuation.

Calligraphy

ta (t) as in *stop.*

Gives wealth and makes others kindly disposed toward
you and your ideas.

Calligraphy

tha (th) as in *hot-house.*

Spiritual attainment.

Calligraphy

da (d) as in *dose.*

Promotes growth and
pleasant circumstances

Calligraphy

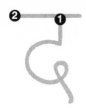

dha (dh) as in *adhoc.*

Mercy, healing, help, gift.

Calligraphy

na (n) as in *nap.*

Tranquility, enjoyment and liberation.

Calligraphy

pa (p) as in *pot.*

Authority, devotion, protection,
auspicious. Removes obstacles.

Calligraphy

pha (ph) as in *up hill.*

Protection, authority, devotion,
affecting the astral and etheric matrix,
helps to develop siddhis.

Calligraphy

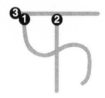

ba (b) as in *bat.*

The manifest power of Shiva - Shakti, yin and yang, the full moon. Used to project energy and force and to materialize thoughts and feelings.
Destroys negativity.

Calligraphy

bha (bh) as in *rub hard.*

Same as *ba* but affecting the astral etheric matrix.
Destroyer of worldliness.

Calligraphy

ma (m) as in *moon.*

Magnetic, nurturing energy,
attractive power, mesmerizing.

Calligraphy

ya (y) as in *yes.*

Inspiration, intuition, yoga,
air element.

Calligraphy

ra (r) as in *run.*

Heat, energy, fire element.

Calligraphy

la (l) as in *love.*

Cohesion, stability, earth element.

Calligraphy

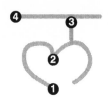

va (v) as in *vine.*

Receptivity, intuition, magnetism, nurturing,
water element.

Calligraphy

śa (sh) as in *ship.*

Gives success.

Calligraphy

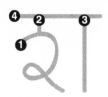

ṣa *(sh)* as in *shine.*

Gives wealth and fulfilment
of desires.

Calligraphy

sa (s) as in **sun.**

Root of knowledge.

Calligraphy

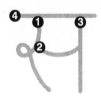

ha (h) as in *home.*

The power of the word. Akasha. Gives knowledge.

Calligraphy

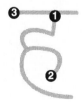

kṣa (ksh) as in *action.*

Gives knowledge in all realms,
spiritual and material.

Calligraphy

The Seed Mantras - Bíja

ॐ , ओँ *or* औँ
Oṁ (Om) or Auṁ (Aum)

Pranava, **Oṁ,** is the matrix for all manifestation and the well, so to speak, from which all water comes. Recognizing this gives power to thought and speech and creates mantra. Any word or sentence spoken in Sanskrit is a mantra if it is understood to be a mantra; and any word or sentence spoken in any language is also a mantra, but much less potent than when spoken in Sanskrit because of Sanskrit's direct connection to prana. Any word or sentence in Sanskrit or any other language, prefixed with **Oṁ** will turn that utterance into a mantra.

The *Mantra Yoga Samhita* states, "**Oṁ** is the crest jewel among all the mantras," and, "all mantras achieve their full prowess from **Oṁ**." It also states, "**Oṁ** is pronounced for the siddhi of all the mantras; therefore **Oṁ** is undoubtedly lord of all the mantras."

To understand what **Oṁ** is in relation to other mantras, consider **Oṁ** to be an electrical outlet and the other mantras are different appliances that can be plugged into that outlet. In order to make the appliances work, they need a source of power. That is the **Oṁ**.

To further the analogy, you need a specific appliance to do the job needed. If you need light, you plug in a lamp; if you need to clean the floors, you plug in a vacuum cleaner. Mantras are like the appliances in that each is configured in Sanskrit to route the energy in a certain way to produce the phenomenon desired. You use the same energy but each mantra is a template which configures the energy to produce specific results. When plugged into the *Oṁ* source, any mantra will be powered by and enlivened by that source to perform the tasks in accord with its dharma.

इँ

Īṁ (Eem)

This mantra makes pranava manifest in the environment that we currently inhabit, so essentially it makes the transcendant apparent in the immanent. It also transmits pranava to the world around us, or to a specific person or location, and so is a blessing of enlightenment. It can be suffixed to other mantras to direct the mantric energy to a specific point in time and space. This mantra is often used by gurus to transmit knowledge and experience to students.

ह्रीँ

Hrīṁ (Hreem)

This mantra is maya/illusion or the phenomenal world as we know it. It evokes illusion and manifests or dissolves it, depending on what is added to this bija. The phrase "it's all done with smoke and mirrors" relates to this mantra in that it will reveal the hidden workings that create the illusion.

ऐं

Aiṁ (Aym)

This is the guru and Saraswati bija. Saraswati is the goddess of knowledge, music, arts and science. Guru is that which dispells *avidya* (ignorance). Guru is our guide, teacher and protector, and resides within us in our sahasrara. Chanting this bija brings knowledge, skill and your guru (inward or outward) to you according to your needs.

श्रीं

Śrīṁ (Shreem)

This is the bija of Lakshmi, goddess of wealth, abundance and comfort and pleasure. This bija is said to open up pathways to prosperity, luck, pleasantries and magnetic charm. Lakshmi is the cosmic principle of generosity, kindness, nurture, satisfaction and contentment. Chanting this bija is auspicious for many endeavors.

क्रीं

Krīṁ (Kreem)

This is the bija of Kali. The goddess Kali represents form as time and space in its three modes: creation, preservation and dissolution. Chanting this mantra reveals the underpinnings of the universe and gives the understanding of cycles and their significance. This mantra grants siddhis and great wisdom.

हल्रीँ

Hlrīṁ (Hlreem)

and

हलीँ

Hlīṁ (Hleem)

This mantra stops and slows actions, dependng on your intent. If you are the recipient of negative energy, no matter what the source, this mantra will stop that energy in its tracks. This works for both internal as well as external problems.

हुँ

Huṁ (Hum)

This mantra repels and protects against harm. It is said to remove negative energy and replace it with your positive intent.

हूँ

Hūṁ (Hoom)

This mantra penetrates and transforms. It protects and repels negative energy, but in a sutle way, creating waves that deflect disharmony. It also informs and, when used internally, allows us to invoke whatever vibration we wish to experience. Similarly when expressed outwardly towards others it will convey to and impregnate people with a sense of openness and receptivity for whatever is conveyed with the mantra. It is a good mantra to use when studying in order to create receptivity and deep learning which will last.

कलीँ

Klīṁ (Kleem)

This is the bija of Kama, god of desire, and can provoke desire in ourselves or others. Chanting this bija creates attraction, arouses passions and feelings of love, and has the magnetism to bring us what we need in life. It also gives an understanding of the law of desire and attraction as it relates to karma and reincarnation.

स्त्रीँ

Strīṁ (Streem)

This mantra broadcasts waves of energy and can be used as a carrier wave for any other mantra to project a feeling or quality. It gives the ability to break away from thought forms (our own and those of others) which weigh us down or prevent us from being free in our thoughts, feelings and actions. It releases us from bondage to samskaras and frees us from negative emotions.

त्रीँ

Trīṁ (Treem)

Breaks the chains of emotional, mental and physical bondage. Destroys oppressive vibrations, allows freedom of movement and helps to pierce the veil of maya.

दुँ

Duṁ (Dum)

This is a Durga mantra which destroys negative energy and protects from harm. It breaks down barriers and opposition to your goals.

दूँ

Dūṁ (Doom)

This Durga mantra annihilates any inimical force aimed at you and destroys any effort by those who wish to prevent you from obtaining moksha.

हौँ

Hauṁ (Howm)

This is a potent healing mantra, a powerful prana tonic for the physical, mental, and astral bodies. It strengthens the aura and deflects the negative effects of disharmony and chaos.

होँ

Hoṁ (Home)

This is a healing mantra used for specific healing tasks in different parts of the physical body, aura, or mental and astral bodies.

सौँ

Sauṁ (Sowm)

This mantra connects to the treasure house of images related to soma and the Moon, and the Milky Way, which is the center of our galaxy. It relates to the revolution of the earth, the deep meaning of the dance of the Sufis, and the myth of the churning of the ocean of milk. It gives us a sense of place in the universe.

सौः

Sauḥ (Sowha)

This mantra stops movement in time and space and allows us to center or meditate on one point in time so that we can examine and understand the esoteric meaning of a certain portion of a distinct cycle. A Sufi dancer centers on a specific moment in time and space and lets it carry them around its circular vortex and back to the source. This meditation can be done with or without physical movement. Tai Chi also uses the principle of this mantra to carry the meditator through the nature of form to reach its cosmic meaning and release its chi or prana power.

हसौः

Hsauḥ (Hsowha)

This mantra impregnates any idea attached to it with prana, which makes it strong and vital in order to stimulate others with that particular idea. It is very good for reviving depleted energy, whether emotional, mental or physical.

ग्लौं

Glaum̐ (Glowm)

This is an auspicious Ganesha mantra that clears the way and grounds our efforts in harmony with the universal matrix and cosmic tides.

क्ष्रौं

Kṣrauṁ (Ksrowm)

This mantra is generally used to weed out those qualities that we do not want in our lives, internally and externally. It is very effective for working with the most stubborn forces and forms that are hard to budge. It helps to stop people and institutions from blocking our path to moksha, which also means happiness, prosperity and health.

रां

Rāṁ (Ram)

This is the mantra of Rama, the perfect ruler, protector and master of dharma. Chanting this mantra gives a sense of what your role is in this lifetime and helps to overcome limitations. It also invokes powers to protect yourself from the machinations of external foes and gives victory over those who would keep you from moksha. It is related to the solar fire element.

मां

Māṁ (Mam)

This mantra, related to the lunar water element, is magnetic, creates attraction and harmony, and preserves and protects. It is nurturing and brings beneficial circumstances into your life. In a difficult situations, this mantra helps to restore balance and give comfort and ease.

Miscellaneous Mantras

हुं फट् स्वाहा
Huṁ Phaṭ Svāhā (Hum Phat Svaha)

This mantra is used to dispel and destroy negative forces that attempt to impinge on your life and keep you from moksha. It is very protective and deflects ill intention from people and institutions as well as demons on all planes of existence.

हंसः सोऽहं
Haṁsaḥ So'haṁ (Hamsa So'ham)

This mantra balances the solar and lunar forces within us and helps us to connect with our higher self. It helps us to see the interplay of opposites in our lives so that we can intuit what we need, and how to move and flow through time and space. It is usually coupled with pranayama, but does not have to be.

नमः
Namaḥ (Namaha)

When suffixed to any deity mantra, it opens us up and tunes us in to that deity's essence. It is a vibration of respect and reverence. When suffixed to any mantra, the knowledge of that mantra will flood into your consiousness, and enliven and enlighten you with its presence.

स्वाहा
Svāhā (Svaha)

This mantra suffix transforms all actions into the intended result of the main mantra. It sacrifices ritual activities such as japa to the necessary causal energy that can then re-manifest in the form we desire.

जै
Jai (Jy)
and
जय
Jaya (Jaya)

Each of these mantras can be added at the end of any spoken word, speech, mantra, etc., to obtain success and victory in what has been spoken.

हरि ओँ
Hari Oṁ (Hari Om)

This mantra evokes the golden white light contained within form, and thus enlightenment. It is an avatar (such as Krishna) mantra and evokes the avatar's presence and blessing. An excellent mantra for general protection.

ॐ तत् सत्
Oṁ Tat Sat

This mantra is often used to end a discourse. It means "absolute truth," "so be it," or "what is," and is often used to end other mantras. It helps to materialize the effects desired.

ॐ शान्ति
Oṁ Śānti

This is the mantra of peace and serenity. It transforms us and our surrounds, and dispells discordant vibrations.

Deities & Mantra

In *Sanatana Dharma* (eternal nature or law), or Hinduism as it is more popularly known, there are many deities, all of which represent some aspect of the one truth. It is much like looking at a cut gemstone. Although there are many facets, it is still one stone. In Buddhism, this same idea is expressed by the mantra *Oṁ Maṇi Padme Hūṁ*, "Hail to the jewel in the lotus," - one jewel, a thousand petals.

The vajra of Indra

The magical object connected to this mantra is the vajra of Indra and is called in Buddhism the diamond scepter. The diamond scepter is related to the diamond body, forever unchangeable but with many facets.

The facets of the jewel in one sense are the deities who are time-space symbols of energies that are connected with particular physical, emotional and mental phenomenon. Representations of these deities are present in most rituals as a focal point for in-drawing, out-drawing and dispersion of their respective energies.

At the simplest level, every time you see a picture or statue of Lakshmi you think of wealth, abundance and other attributes associated with that goddess. This sets up a current

Lakshmi

of energy with you as part of the circuit. Concepts and feelings related to Lakshmi become integrated into your thoughts and feelings. You become more conscious of all that is connected with Laksmi, and you receive the benefits she can bestow. It is like tuning a radio to a particular frequency.

Deities are conglomerates of specific forces - a few petals of the lotus, or facets of the diamond. We ourselves are also conglomerates of forces. These force fields consist of electrons, protons, neutrons or whatever you would like to call them, and they are all directed by thought.

Carl Jung called deities "archetypes." Each archetype is given a particular form by each culture that may differ in details of representation but in fact serve as a contact point for the same energies and entities. Once a form is designated to represent a certain complex of energies, it becomes alive and answers to its name and form just as we do when our name is called. The reality of a deity is just as viable as the reality of you. Every person is a sort of a theme park or a story that has its own mythology and real live action.

At the most macrocosmic level, the deities of Sanatana Dharma are aspects of the one Brahman. Most deities are presented in an anthropomorphic, zoomorphic or combination form, but they are also represented by geometric figures in yantras

Ganesha yantra

and mandalas, pentagrams, hexagrams, circles, triangles, etc. Relating to these archetypal energies via geometry is equally as effective as using human, animal or plant forms for deities. It is simply a matter of preference.

Deity forms are interfaces for complexes of energy which are also related to the elements, and the planets, and other celestial and terrestrial phenomenon. Worship or puja is simply conversation and interaction with these forces.

Puja is the act of focussing consciousness on a deity and its energy matrix. It should be understood that the attitude of puja is quite different from the Christian attitude of worship. The word "worship" is only used here to approach the concept of puja for westerners.

Ganesha

Acts of puja - for instance, recitation of "the thousand names" of a deity - create concentration and focus of thought and feeling, much like a magnifying glass co-heres sunlight into a tiny burning point. Such focused, coherent energy, like a laser beam, is quite powerful when used to produce certain re-sults or fulfill certain needs.

Shiva

Deity mantras

Shiva Mantra. Evokes Shiva and is a potent mantra for protection. It destroys negative vibrations within and without.

ॐ नमः शिवाय
Oṁ Namaḥ Śivāya

Ganesha Mantra. This mantra breaks down barriers and obstacles in our journey to moksha. It clears a path through the thickets of life so that we may have success with what we wish to accomplish.

ॐ गं गणपतये नमः
Oṁ Gaṁ Gaṇapataye Namaḥ

Ganesha Mantra. This mantra, like the preceeding Ganesha mantra, is a remover of obstacles, whether mental, emotional or physical.

ॐ गं गणेशाय नमः

Oṁ Gaṁ Gaṇeṣaya Namaḥ

Lakshmi Mantra. Lakshmi brings wealth and comfort, prosperity and abundance. This mantra also bestows happiness, love, contentment, beauty and harmony.

ॐ श्रीं लक्षमयै नमः

Oṁ Śrīṁ Lakṣmyai Namaḥ

Mrityunjaya Bija Mantra. This is the short seed syllable version of a powerful and very popular Shiva healing mantra.

ॐ हौं जूं सः

Oṁ Hauṁ Jūṁ Saḥ

Honor to Narayan. This mantra puts you in tune with the universe, dissolves disharmony and confers liberation from *avidya* (ignorance). It connects us with enlightened sentient life forms throughout the cosmos and contains within it the secret of the music of the spheres.

ॐ नमे नारायणाय

Oṁ Namo Nārāyanāya

Brahma Mantra. This mantra unites us with Brahma, the creative principle. It is often used to begin a discourse or project. It means "I am Brahma" and thus awakens us to our creative powers.

ॐ अहम ब्रहम अस्मि

Oṁ Aham Brahma Asmi

Kali Mantra. Evokes Kali, and gives the sadhaka a deep understanding of the nature of time and space and thus all universal processes at any level. It will reveal to you, if you so desire, the nature of karma and how to transcend and transform karma.

ॐ काली

Oṁ Kālī

Mantras of the Five Elements

The five elements are a major component of Tantric cosmology, and are the building blocks of our phenomenal universe, including other dimensions of time and space. Everything in the universe, which of course includes our thoughts and feelings, are composed of these elements. Each element and combination of elements has a specific vibratory rate and thus a sound - a mantra.

Each letter of the Sanskrit alphabet, and all the combinations of the letters, have specific effects due to their inherent elemental vibration. Gods and goddesses also have specific vibratory rates and are complex combinations of the elements, representing detailed ideas, feelings and manifestations.

The balance and transmutation of the elements through mantra sadhana is the centerpiece of Tantric practice. The personality characteristics of the elements are important to learn so that you can discover which elements predominate and which are lacking in your psychic makeup. Once you know this, you can then chant the mantra of the lacking element to create more balance in your personality.

Vamacharin's wand for working
with the five elements

98

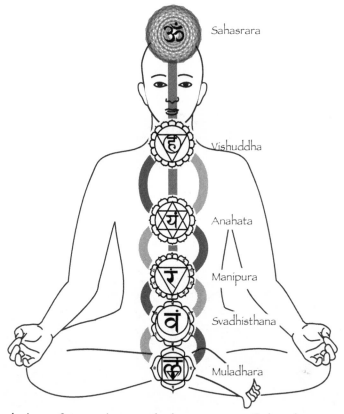

Chakras for working with the mantras of the elements

For instance, if you have a lot of fire in your makeup, which can sometimes make you too aggressive, you can chant a water element mantra to balance out the fire.

In addition to working on your personal samskaras, you can chant mantras to evoke the elements simply to experience them and learn about them. One way to do this is to transfer your consciousness into the chakra of the element you want to experience and chant the mantra for that element. While chanting the mantra, visualize the color of the element and imagine the sensation that goes with it, such as heat for the fire element and coolness for water, and so forth. This will bring you into close contact with the element and give you knowledge of its essential nature.

Mūlādhāra - मूलाधार

Pṛthivī - पृथिवी *- Earth*   *Bija -* ल *- La*

The earth element limits consciousness to form but also gives us the ability to use objects and form to transcend our limitations, as in the use of ritual objects. The qualities of earth are gravity, weight, density, and cohesion. It is yin, magnetic and in-drawing. The color of earth varies from one region to another, so for visualization, imagine whatever color of soil you are familiar with, and a feeling of heaviness and gravity. You can transfer your consciousness to the deepest caverns of the earth and become one with the earth element.

Business, money, employment, practical affairs are all related to the element of earth. It bestows endurance, conscientiousness, respect and responsibility and represents the quality of omnipresence. Too much earth produces laziness, lack of conscience, melancholy, and dullness.

Svādhiṣṭhāna - स्वाधिष्ठान

Āpas - आपस् - *Water*   *Bija* - व - *Va*

The water element rules emotions and feeling, and gives keen perceptions into the myriad forms of life and their interaction. It is yin, magnetic, receptive, in-drawing and attractive. It is related to the divine quality of immortality. It produces feelings of pleasure and happiness; and enhances compassion, tranquility, tenderness and forgiveness. Too much water produces shyness, and can make one over-compliant, or negligent.

When chanting the water mantra, visualize the color blue-green and feel the coolness of the element in your imagination. You can transfer your consciousness into a lake, pond, river or ocean and immerse yourself; and/or actually sit in water while you perform the mantra. You can also meditate upon the power of great waterfalls like Niagara, or the Moon and the tides.

Maṇipūra - मणिपूर

Tejas - तेजस् - Fire   *Bija - र - Ra*

The fire element mantra bestows courage, activity, energy. It is yang, electric in nature and outgoing. It is light and vision, color and visualization. If you feel blocked and need impetus to move forward, meditation using the fire element mantra works well. The fire element enhances the will and visual perceptions, and gives enthusiasm, power, dominion, authority, and prestige. It is related to the divine quality omnipotence. Too much fire can create jealousy, vindictiveness, and anger; and should be balanced out with the element of water.

When chanting the fire mantra, visualize the color red. Imagine feeling heat and expansion, and the brightness of the light given off by fire; or transfer your consciousness to the center of the sun, or to any fire such as a candle flame, and become one with it.

The siddhi most often associated with the element of fire is the ability to produce heat in the body such as some Tibetan monks do in the practice of tumo. Mastery of the fire element allows the lighting of any combustable material. Some Tantrics light ritual fires with the fire mantra.

Anāhata - अनाहत

Vāyu - वायु *- Air*   *Bija -* य *- Ya*

The air element bestows joy, kindness, optimism, a keen intellect and a sensitive ear. It is yang, electric in nature and outgoing; related to the divine quality of omniscience and wisdom; and enhances hearing, reason, and logic. It is the word and thus rules mantra.

Too much air produces frivolity, self-presumption, boasting, squandering, gossiping. To balance out negative air traits, chant the earth mantra.

When chanting the air mantra, visualize a light sky-blue color, and imagine your body becoming very light. One form of air meditation is to look up at the sky, close your eyes and rise up into the sky and become one with it. Feel the breeze, the wind, the hurricane, the tornado. Feel light as air and imagine there is no gravity. The siddhi most often associated with the element of air is levitation.

Viśuddha - विशुद्ध

Ākāśa - आकाश *- Ether*   *Bija -* ह *- Ha*

Akasha is timeless and spaceless, and called the fifth power. Its active symbol is the five-pointed star or pentagram, and its meditation symbol is the bindu or point. It is the element from which the other four are derived, and the essence of everything which is nothing, and which contains all. It is the power behind mantra and represents our self-preservation instinct and conscience. The Tantric phrase, "What is here is there, what is not here is not there," is the essence of understanding akasha. When chanting the akasha mantra, visualize the color violet or ultraviolet and imagine that you are the center of, and connected to every point in infinite space.

Raising Kundalini

In practice, the mantras of the elements can be combined in many ways to produce different effects.

The core practice of Tantra is raising kundalini. Each element mantra is assigned to a specific chakra, and is the key to unlocking that chakra to allow kundalini energy to flow through it.

Method 1

To raise kundalini, begin by transferring your consciousness to the muladhara chakra and chanting the prithivi mantra *La* once. Then rise up your spine within the sushumna channel to the svadhisthana chakra and chant the apas mantra *Va*. Next move up to the manipura chakra and chant the tejas *Ra* mantra once; then to the anahata with *Ya*; then in vishuddha chant *Ha*. From vishuddha, move up to sahasrara above your head and chant *Oṁ*.

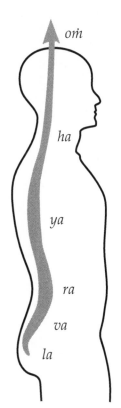

ल व र य ह ॐ
La Va Ra Ya Ha Oṁ

When raising the kundalini with this technique, you do not pass through the ajna (at the front of the head between the eyebrows) or chandra (the soft spot at the top of the neck just below the skull on the back of your neck) chakras as you might with techniques for other purposes.

Rise up the spine on the in-breath and feel the kundalini being pulled up through the action of your breathing. At the sahasrara, exhale, then transfer your consciousness back down to the muladhara and resume the cycle over and over again, continually transferring and transmuting your consciousness upwards.

Chanting the mantras in the chakras is done in the mind, but to prepare the physical body you can chant the mantras physically out loud for as many repetitions as you like; to prepare the astral body, whisper the mantras. The final practice of raising kundalini is generally chanted in the mind silently.

Although this is an easy mantra cycle, you may wish to work with a teacher who can guide you at first. A teacher is not necessary but can be helpful.

There are many variations on this core mantra cycle. Some techniques are coupled with pranayama or not depending on the teacher and school. The different techniques functionally overlap, but have a different range of effects upon the consciousness.

When moving up the chakras to raise the kundalini, the elemental bija (seed syllable) does not end with a bindu - the nasal *ṁ* sound. The bija ends with the vowel, the short *a* sound as in the word "another." This gives it a more active yang vibration.

Method 2

When the bindu nasal *ṁ* sound is added to the bija mantra, it becomes more magnetic, yin, receptive in nature and creates a different effect. For instance, in the following technique, elemental bija mantras with the bindu ending are used in each chakra, rising from muladhara to sahasrara.

ॐ लं हूँ   ॐ वं हूँ   ॐ रं हूँ

Oṁ Laṁ Hūṁ, Oṁ Vaṁ Hūṁ, Oṁ Raṁ Hūṁ,

ॐ यं हूँ   ॐ हं हूँ   ॐ क्षं हूँ   ॐ ओं हूँ

Oṁ Yaṁ Hūṁ, Oṁ Haṁ Hūṁ, Oṁ Kṣaṁ Hūṁ,
Oṁ Oṁ Hūṁ

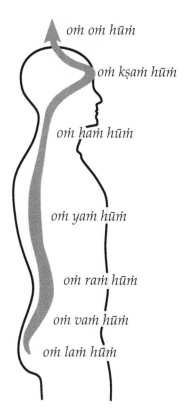

oṁ oṁ hūṁ

oṁ kṣaṁ hūṁ

oṁ haṁ hūṁ

oṁ yaṁ hūṁ

oṁ raṁ hūṁ

oṁ vaṁ hūṁ

oṁ laṁ hūṁ

Note that this cycle does pass through the ajna, while the first technique does not.

This mantra cycle floods the chakras with soma to provide a matrix through which the kundalini can rise. It prepares the fields of the chakras and balances consciousness in each chakra, paving the way, so to speak, for kundalini to rise, although in some sense it is actually kundalini rising to prepare a way for itself.

Method 3

Another variation is to prefix each elemental bija mantra with the akasha bija mantra while ascending through the chakras. The intoned sequence is

हल हव हर हय हह हओं
HaLa, HaVa, HaRa, HaYa, HaHa, HaOṁ

from muladhara to sahasrara, going directly from vishudda to sahasrara without going through the ajna. This puts your consciousness into the akasha/sushumna/chitrini channel and allows kundalini to rise unhindered. The akasha mantra evokes akasha to balance the ida and pingala channels (the lunar and solar forces respectively) on each side of each chakra. This is important because kundalini does not rise until the chakra is balanced in bindu.

ha oṁ

ha ha

ha ya

ha ra

ha va

ha la

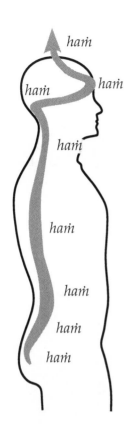

Method 4

हं

Ham

The akasha mantra can be used by it-self with the added bindu nasal *ṁ* sound (anusvara), *haṁ*, in each chakra from muladhara to sahasrara, in this case including both chandra and ajna chakras. The function is very much like Method 3 in that akasha is used to balance each chakra.

ॐ

Once the fields are prepared and the energies are balanced, the seed syllables of the elements can be planted, and the lotus of the chakra, with its petals, unfolds.

Timing for Mantra

When discussing time and timing for mantra, we are referring to cycles and planetary relationships - in other words, astrology more than clock time. While it is beyond the scope of this book to go into astrology in depth, those unfamiliar with astrology may benefit from learning and observing some very basic astrological cycles.

Solar (daily and annual) and lunar cycles are a good place to begin the study of how mantra works with astrology.

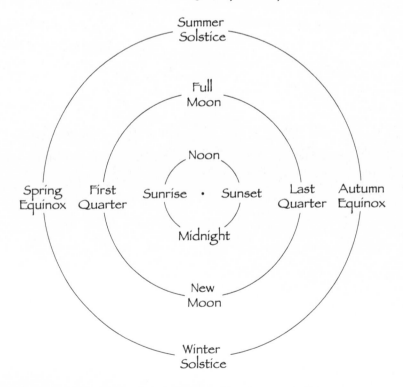

Solar and lunar cycle quarter points

The most basic division of these cycles is into quarters which are:

🕉 *Daily cycle* - sunrise, noon, sunset and midnight;

🕉 *Monthly cycle* - First Quarter, Full Moon, Last Quarter and New Moon;

🕉 *Yearly cycle* - Spring Equinox, Summer Solstice, Fall Equinox and Winter Solstice.

The quarter points are excellent times for chanting mantra, although there are many other points in these and other cycles which are auspicious for chanting specific mantras. Many of these points in the cycles relate to deities and their activities.

For instance, astrologically, the exact moment of the New Moon (*Amavasya*) is the element akasha, and thus a bindu (balance) point. It is also when Shiva/Sun and Shakti/Moon come together in *maithuna* (sexual intercourse), and manifest bindu. The New Moon is not visible and, as akasha, it is the gateway to *nirguna* Brahman (Brahman without attributes). Akasha, unlike the other four elements, is timeless and spaceless; and it is the source of other four elements.

The full moon (*Purnima*) is the symbol of *saguna* Brahman (Brahman with attributes) as the moon is totally visible.

The relationship between Sun and Moon, the cycle of lunar phases, is very important.

The total lunar cycle is a mirror-like reflection of Kali, who, through the actions of Shiva and Shakti, reveals herself in the birth, maturation and death of ideas, emotions and objects, at all levels of existence in the phenomenal world.

One way the Hindu lunar calendar divides the lunar cycle is into 30 lunar days, or *tithis*, of 12 degrees each. The tithis are one of the factors used to delineate the best times to chant specific mantras and to perform other actions of importance.

Generally, mantras for earthly matters are performed during the waxing (New Moon to Full Moon) phase, referred to as *shukla paksha* (bright fortnight), culminating in saguna Brahman. Mantras for spiritual matters are performed during the waning phase (Full Moon to New Moon), known as *krishna paksha* (dark fortnight) as the cycle returns to nirguna Brahman.

Gharis

Another cycle to note is the daily cycle of *gharis*, 30 divisions of more or less 24 minutes each from sunrise to sunset, and sunset to sunrise. For chanting mantras to work with a particular *tattwa* (element), it is helpful to choose a corresponding ghari for timing your mantra practice.

Each ghari is ruled by one of the five elements - akasha, air, fire, water, earth; in that sequence - from sunrise to sunset. The cycle begins again at sunset with the same sequence. Each ghari lasts for roughly 24 minutes, but of course, the length varies according to the exact time of sunrise and sunset.

To calculate which element is in force at any given time, look up the times of sunset and sunrise for the day in question. The exact times of sunrise and sunset for your location for a particular day, or for an entire year can be found at the U.S. Naval Observatory web site. To calculate the gharis, simply figure out how many minutes it is between sunrise and sunset for that particular day. Divide this into 30 sections and you will have the length of each ghari. The first ghari (at sunrise or sunset) will be akasha. This is followed in order by air, fire, water, and earth. This sequence repeats itself until sunset. At sunset, begin again with akasha, followed by air, fire, water, and earth as during the day. For the whole day you would have twelve sets of tattwas.

Planetary hours

The tables mentioned above can also be used to calculate planetary hours if you do not have an astrological program that has this feature.

Planetary hours are calculated from sunrise and sunset, but the sequence of the planets depends on the day of the week. For instance, the Sun rules Sunday and so the first planetary hour would be ruled by the Sun. On Monday the first planetary hour would be the Moon, because Monday is ruled by the Moon. Similarly Saturn rules Saturday, Venus rules Friday, Jupiter rules Thursday, Mercury rules Wednesday, and Mars rules Tuesday.

The sequence of the planetary hours is always this: Sun ☉, Venus ♀, Mercury ☿, Moon ☽, Saturn ♄, Jupiter ♃, Mars ♂. Each day starts at sunrise with the planet of the day and moves through the sequence. Unlike the gharis, the sequence of planetary hours continues through sunset and does not begin anew.

To calculate the length of each planetary hour, calculate how many minutes there are from sunrise to sunset and divide this number by twelve. The night hours are calculated the same way, except using the minutes from sunset to sunrise to create twelve divisions. Thus, there are 24 planetary hours in a day.

Planetary cycles

At a more complex level are the planetary cycles: planetary positions and aspects (angles of relationship). The planet Mercury rules mantra in general, and one of the most important astrological considerations for mantra is whether the planet Mercury is in direct or retrograde motion. A planet in retrograde seems to move backwards because of the position of the Earth in relation to the retrograde planet as they both orbit the Sun. It is most ideal to start chanting a new mantra when Mercury's motion is direct, and avoid the retrograde period, which usually last about three weeks. Mercury retrogrades are listed in any astrological ephemeris and these periods can easily be found online.

Each planet rules certain endeavors, and it is auspicious to begin practice of particular mantras intended to address some issue at hand during a good aspect of Mercury to the planet that rules the issue.

Timing and astrological considerations are not necessary in mantra practice, but it can speed the process significantly to flow with certain cosmic tides rather than to swim against them. Any study of either Vedic or western astrology will be beneficial. Ultimately, as you practice mantra, the practice itself and the intuition you gain in the process will automatically guide you to the best times to do things.

Planetary Mantras

Astrology gives us an indication of cosmic forces at work. Each planet is a glyph in the astrological alphabet that is connected with particular areas of our lives, inwardly and outwardly.

The Tantric axiom "What is here is there. What is not here is not there," and the Hermetic axiom "As above, so below," show a way to understand the stellar story book.

It is said, and should be understood, that "the stars incline, they do not compel." Planetary configurations are expressions of particular types of cosmic energy that create tendencies towards certain types of events, actions and reactions in a person's life. Those who are unaware of these energy flows are most likely simply swept along in the currents. But, by paying attention to the cosmic cycles it is possible to work with the energy flows.

Traditonally, the system of western astrology is relatively light on "remedies," meaning specific ways to work with the planetary cycles to mitigate or enhance planetary effects. Not so in jyotish (vedic astrology). Indian astrology is rich in remedies, including mantra and the making of talismans.

Planetary mantras are intended to manifest the blessings and good fortune of the planets, and smooth out or negate difficult planetary influences. Chanting the mantras of the planets on a daily or weekly basis will help to improve circumstances.

The student of mantra should also study astrology.

Sun/Sūrya
ॐ ह्रीं सूरयाय नमः
Oṁ Hrīṁ Sūryāya Namaḥ

The Sun rules our ego self, our will power, our presence on the stage of life. It represents vitality and vital interests, indicates our birthright and bestows authority. It is our self expression. The zodiacal sign position of the Sun in our birth chart indicates what type of deity we most readily relate to. The Sun is life giving, healing and outgoing.

Moon/Candra
ॐ श्रीं चानदराय नमः
Oṁ Śrīṁ Candrāya Namaḥ

The Moon rules subconscious forces and tendencies from past incarnations, and our habits and moods. It rules domestic harmony, motherhood, children, home and hearth, and that which nourishes and protects. The Moon indicates our receptivity to the world and our capability for empathy and nurturing. It is magnetic and receptive.

☿ Mercury/Budha

ॐ बरीं बुदहाय नमः

Oṁ Brīṁ Budhāya Namaḥ

Mercury is the messenger of the gods and as such relates to the ability to order the mind in preparation for meditation. It rules the gift of oratory and writing and other forms of communication, education and knowledge, and most of all, mantra. It relates to our ability to think and understand ideas; and make connections between exoteric symbols and their esoteric meaning. It represents the nature and quality of our ongoing dialogue with the universe and the script for the play of our life.

♀ Venus/Śukra

ॐ दरीं शुकराय नमः

Oṁ Drīṁ Śukrāya Namaḥ

Venus rules our ability to attract and love and harmonize. It gives refinement of senses and an appreciation for beauty and adornment at an inner as well as outer level. It is harmony and wealth and happiness. Venus brings peace, rest, pleasure, and comfort. It is magnetic, attractive, receptive.

♂ ## Mars/Kuja

ॐ क्रीं कुजाय नमः

Oṁ Krīṁ Kujāya Namaḥ

Mars is outgoing. It rules the ability to act, and energizes us. It relates to the principle of self-preservation and gives the power of a warrior to fight and struggle forward against extreme odds. It provides healing and heating energy to our auras.

♃ ## Jupiter/Bṛhaspati

ॐ गरीं गुरवे नमः

Oṁ Grīṁ Gurave Namaḥ

Jupiter rules the concept of guru and the nature of our religious, spiritual or philosophical self. It is the ritual we bind ourselves to in order to proceed further in our evolutionary path; and the expansion of consciousness that allows us to understand the laws of the universe beyond our ego-limited perspective. It is related to the concepts of divine providence and grace. It is outgoing, electric and relates to the element of fire.

♄ Saturn/Śani
ॐ परीं शनये नमः
Oṁ Prīṁ Śanaye Namaḥ

Saturn rules the concepts of maya and karma, and thus form and form's movement in time and space. Saturn's rings are called rings-pass-not as they represent the boundary of the illusory world that we have to transcend in order to reach moksha/liberation.

☊ Rāhu/North Node of Moon
ॐ बहरीं राहवे नमः
Oṁ Bhrīṁ Rāhave Namaḥ

☋ Ketu/South Node of Moon
ॐ स्त्रीं केतवे नमः
Oṁ Strīṁ Ketave Namaḥ

The North Node of the Moon and the South Node of the Moon are said to represent challenges that occur on our spiritual path; thus, they lead us to the skills we need to acquire in order to complete that path in this lifetime.

The other planets in our solar system such as Uranus, Neptune, Pluto are not mentioned in classical mantra literature as they were not discovered and thus not in our consciousness until 1781, 1846 and 1930 respectively. Their effects are directly related to magic, mysticism and transmutation. Although yogis, magicians and mystics have been aware of these vibrations for thousands of years, humanity has only recently begun the process of integrating the vibrations of these three planets and to work with them consciously.

It is said by some that:

⛢ **Uranus**

The god Indra is related to Uranus, thus any mantra to Indra will have that planetary vibration.

♆ **Neptune**

The god Varuna is related to Neptune and any mantra to Varuna will have that planetary vibration.

♇ **Pluto**

The god Yama is related to Pluto and any mantra to Yama will have that planetary vibration. Note that recently Pluto was downgraded from planet to dwarf planet status by the International Astronomical Union, however this downgrade is of no consequence to astrologers who still consider Pluto a planet to reckon with.

Directional Mantras

Vastu is the Hindu science of architecture, space and environment. It employs the esoteric understanding of the five elements and astrological energies, and how these operate through the compass directions. Vastu is similar to Feng Shui in the way that it helps us to harmoniously align with the energies that move through and around us in our environment.

According to Vastu, our physical world is permeated with subtle energies that align in particular patterns in three dimensional space. So, by delineating the space around us, one can tune into and work with these subtle energies. Vastu delineates space into ten directions.

Each direction has a deity which can be called upon for protection from negative influences and to evoke the positive influences that flow from that particular subtle energy. Each directional deity has their own special magical weapon called an astra, and there is a mantra for each deity and astra.

The directional mantras:

East

Deity

ॐ लं इन्द्राय नमः

Oṁ Laṁ Indrāya Namaḥ

Astra

ॐ वं वज्राय नमः

Oṁ Vaṁ Vajrāya Namaḥ

Southeast

Deity

ॐ रं अग्नये नमः

Oṁ Raṁ Agnaye Namaḥ

Astra

ॐ शं शक्तये नमः

Oṁ Śaṁ Śaktaye Namaḥ

South

Deity

ॐ मां यमाय नमः

Oṁ Māṁ Yamāya Namaḥ

Astra

ॐ दं दण्डाय नमः

Oṁ Daṁ Daṇḍāya Namaḥ

Southwest

Deity

ॐ क्षं नैरृत्ये नमः

Oṁ Kṣaṁ Nairṛtaye Namaḥ

Astra

ॐ खं खड्गाय नमः

Oṁ Khaṁ Khaḍgāya Namaḥ

West

Deity

ॐ वं वरुणाय नमः

Oṁ Vaṁ Varuṇāya Namaḥ

Astra

ॐ पं पाशाय नमः

Oṁ Paṁ Pāśāya Namaḥ

Northwest

Deity

ॐ यं वायवे नमः

Oṁ Yaṁ Vāyave Namaḥ

Astra

ॐ अं अंकुशाय नमः

Oṁ Aṁ Aṅkuśāya Namaḥ

North

Deity

ॐ सौं सोमाय नमः

Oṁ Sauṁ Somāya Namaḥ

Astra

ॐ गं गदाय नमः

Oṁ Gaṁ Gadāya Namaḥ

Northeast

Deity

ॐ हं ईशानाय नमः

Oṁ Haṁ Īśānāya Namaḥ

Astra

ॐ तरीं त्रिशूलाय नमः

Oṁ Trīṁ Triśūlāya Namaḥ

Above/Sky

Deity

ॐ आं बरहमणे नमः

Oṁ Āṁ Brahmaṇe Namaḥ

Astra

ॐ पं पदमाय नमः

Oṁ Paṁ Padmāya Namaḥ

Below/Earth

Deity

ॐ ह्रीं अनन्ताय नमः

Oṁ Hrīṁ Anantāya Namaḥ

Astra

ॐ चं चकराय नमः

Oṁ Caṁ Cakrāya Namaḥ

These mantras negate harmful influences and produce beneficial influences from all directions. They can be used in any space at any time to protect and bring peace and blessings. You can protect your home or work space, or any space you wish by reciting the directional mantras in that space on a daily or weekly basis, depending on your inclination.

Begin the mantras facing East and recite the mantra for the deity of the East, and the mantra for the weapon of that deity. Then turn clockwise to face the next compass point and recite the deity and weapon mantras for that direction. Continue clockwise through the Northeast and then recite the mantras for the space above you; and finish with the below / earth mantras.

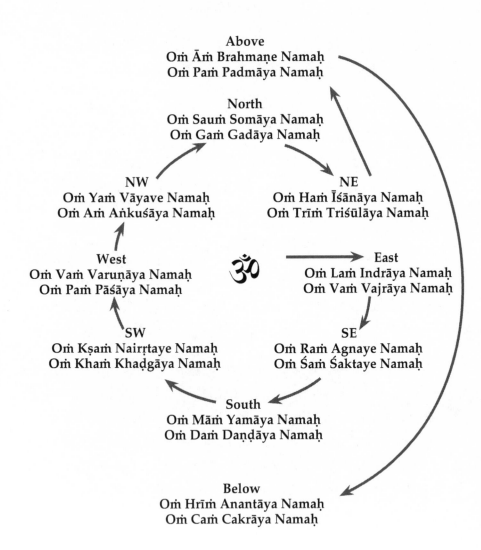

Above
Oṁ Āṁ Brahmaṇe Namaḥ
Oṁ Paṁ Padmāya Namaḥ

North
Oṁ Sauṁ Somāya Namaḥ
Oṁ Gaṁ Gadāya Namaḥ

NW
Oṁ Yaṁ Vāyave Namaḥ
Oṁ Aṁ Aṅkuśāya Namaḥ

NE
Oṁ Haṁ Īśānāya Namaḥ
Oṁ Trīṁ Triśūlāya Namaḥ

West
Oṁ Vaṁ Varuṇāya Namaḥ
Oṁ Paṁ Pāśāya Namaḥ

East
Oṁ Laṁ Indrāya Namaḥ
Oṁ Vaṁ Vajrāya Namaḥ

SW
Oṁ Kṣaṁ Nairṛtaye Namaḥ
Oṁ Khaṁ Khaḍgāya Namaḥ

SE
Oṁ Raṁ Agnaye Namaḥ
Oṁ Śaṁ Śaktaye Namaḥ

South
Oṁ Māṁ Yamāya Namaḥ
Oṁ Daṁ Daṇḍāya Namaḥ

Below
Oṁ Hrīṁ Anantāya Namaḥ
Oṁ Caṁ Cakrāya Namaḥ

Kula Akula and
Mantra Rectification

Rectifying the effect of a mantra

It is said that some mantras are not suitable for some people, so it becomes important to neutralize or rectify any harmful effects that could come from a particular person's use of such a mantra. Traditionally there are many rules for selecting suitable mantras as well as discerning whether a mantra is appropriate for the person's vibration or karma at the moment. Many of these formulas use your name or astrological chart as a base to determine what mantras are appropriate for you.

Kula akula

Kula akula is one of the methods for choosing appropriate mantras. It is based on the first letter of one's first name and the first letter of the mantra.

Each letter belongs to a kula (family). Kula akula means literally "family/not family." The family groups are based on the five elements. A letter is harmonious with other letters in the same family group and some other groups; and is either inharmonious or neutral with other family groups.

- ॐ If the letters are harmonious, the person will get good results with the mantra.

- ॐ If the letters are in the same element family, the results will be excellent.

- ॐ If the letters are inharmonious, good results will not come readily.

- ॐ If the letters are neutral, it will be difficult to get any result at all.

PLANET ग्रह *Graha*	ETHER आकाश *Ākāśa*	AIR वायु *Vāyu*	FIRE तेजस् *Tejas*	WATER आपस् *Āpas*	EARTH पृथिवी *Pṛthivī*
☉ सूर्य *Sūrya/Sun*	ल ḷ लृ ḹ अं aṁ	अ a आ ā ए e	इ i ई ī ऐ ai	ऋ ṛ ॠ ṝ औ au	उ u ऊ ū ओ o
☽ चन्द्र *Candra/Moon*	श śa ह ha	य ya ष ṣa	र ra क्ष kṣa	व va स sa	ल la
☿ बुध *Budha/Mercury*	ण ṇa	ट ṭa	ठ ṭha	ढ ḍha	ड ḍa
♀ शुक्र *Śukra/Venus*	ञ ña	च ca	छ cha	झ jha	ज ja
♂ कुज *Kuja/Mars*	ङ ṅa	क ka	ख kha	घ gha	ग ga
♃ बृबृहस्पति *Bṛhaspati/Jupiter*	न na	त ta	थ tha	ध dha	द da
♄ शनि *Śani/Saturn*	म ma	प pa	फ pha	भ bha	ब ba

ELEMENT	HARMONIOUS	NEUTRAL	INHARMONIUS
Ākāśa/Ether	all	none	none
Vāyu/Air	Tejas/Fire Ākāśa/Ether	Āpas/Water	Pṛthivī/Earth
Tejas/Fire	Vāyu/Air Ākāśa/Ether	Pṛthivī/Earth	Āpas/Water
Āpas/Water	Pṛthivī/Earth Ākāśa/Ether	Vāyu/Air	Tejas/Fire
Pṛthivī/Earth	Āpas/Water Ākāśa/Ether	Tejas/Fire	Vāyu/Air

For example, a person with a first name beginning with P who chants a mantra that starts with a Y should get excellent results according to this system, because P is in the kula of the air element, and Y is also in the air kula.

The kula akula tables can also be used to choose and create elemental or planetary mantras for a variety of purposes.

In practice, we have found that the best way to tell if a mantra is suitable for you is to try using it for a time. If a particular sound does not hit you well after giving it a trial, don't use the mantra, or rectify it.

How to rectify a mantra

If a mantra does not feel right to you but you want to use it for the needed effect, you can rectify it with prefix and/or suffix bija mantras. Rectification cancels out any negative effects that may result if you and the mantra are not quite compatible. When the rectified mantra feels right to you, the mantra in that form can be used without detrimental effect.

For rectification, a mantra can be started with the bijas **Hrīṁ** or **Śrīṁ**, or both together; or, begin and end the mantra with the bija **Oṁ**.

Likhita Japa

Mantra japa can be performed by writing Sanskrit mantras in the Devanagari alphabet. As the mantras are written they are usually pronounced out loud, in the mind or whispered. They can also be written without pronouncing them.

Likhita japa calligraphy is an external mantra meditation. The practice reveals the essence of mantra to the calligrapher just as chanting a mantra will.

As you write each letter, you can, if you wish, listen for the sound of the mantra to emanate from the form you have just made. The sequence of strokes to form each letter can vary depending on teachers but the general stroke sequence is listed with each letter in the letter portraits section beginning on page 30.

Mantras can be written on paper and stored at an altar dedicated to what the mantra represents. Traditionally, once a month (or some other chosen time cycle) the paper is set afire in an *agni* (fire) pit or *havan kund*. By ritual burning, the mantras are discharged into akasha where they create the cause that will result in the effect that the mantra is intended to bring about.

Some sadhakas save their notebooks of mantras for years and then install them in cornerstones of temples and other structures, so that the written mantras will emanate their vibrations in the building.

Tibetan prayer flags written in Uchen script are another example of the use of likhita japa. They are exposed to the wind, rain and sun, to slowly dissolve the mantras from the fabric, giving the mantras over to the elements to materialize the mantras' magic.

Likhita japa can also be woven, printed or dyed into fabric or paper as well as written in ink. The letters of the mantra can be formed into shapes that further develop the meaning and potency of the presentation.

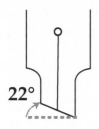

22°

Any type of pen or brush can be used for likhita japa calligraphy, but for a more exacting traditional letter design, use a calligraphy pen nib filed down to the angle shown here, or make a bamboo pen with this angle.

I use a homemade bamboo pen. The nib width should be about 1/8 the height of the characters. You will have

to experiment with this to see how it works for you. The sequence for making a bamboo pen is shown in the photographs. Small diameter bamboo sticks are readily available from online sources and gardening shops. You can also find instructions on the internet for making bamboo pens.

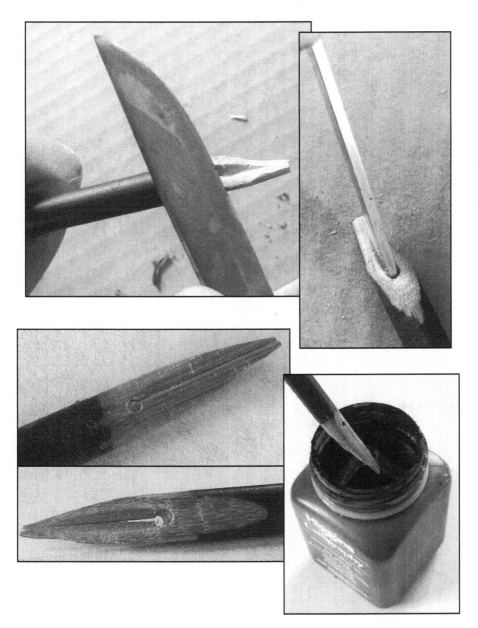

ॐ तत् सत् ओँ

Recommended Reading

Mantra Yoga Samhita. Translated by Ramkumar Rai. Varanasi, India: Chaukhambha Publishers, 2000.

Tantrabhidhana with Vija-Nighantu and Mudra-Nighantu. Edited by Arthur Avalon. New Delhi: Cosmo Publications, 2004.

Lalita. *Choose Your Own Mantra*. New York: Bantam Books, 1978.

Blofeld, John. *Mantras: Sacred Words of Power*. New York: E.P. Dutton & Co., Inc. 1977.

Frawley, David. *Mantra Yoga and Primal Sound: Secrets of Seed (Bija) Mantras*. Twin Lakes, Wisconsin: Lotus Press, 2010.

Swami Satyananda Saraswati, and Swami Vittalananda Saraswati, and Mata Parvatinanda Saraswati. *Laksmi Puja and Thousand Names*. Napa, California: Devi Mandir Publications, 2001.

Bardon, Franz. *The Key to the True Quabbalah*. Wuppertal, West Germany: Dieter Ruggeberg, 1975.

Woodroffe, Sir John. *The Garland of Letters: Studies in the Mantra-Sastra*. Madras, India: Ganesh & Co., 2010

Kundalini Yoga

Hurley, Leigh and Hurley, Phillip. *Tantra, Yoga of Ecstasy: the Sadhaka's Guide to Kundalini and the Left-Hand Path*. Wheelock, Vermont: Maithuna Publications. 2012,

Swami Satyasangananda. *Tattwa Shuddhi*. Munger, Bihar, India: Yoga Publications Trust, 2005.

Goswami Kriyananda. *The Spiritual Science of Kriya Yoga*. Chicago, Illinois: The Temple Of Kriya Yoga, 2006.

Swami Narayanananda. *The Primal Power in Man or the Kundalini Shakti*. Rishikesh, India: Narayanananda Universal Yoga Trust. 1950.

Goswami, Shyam Sundar. *Layayoga: the Definitive Guide to the Chakras and Kundalini*. Rochester, Vermont: Inner Traditions, 1999.

Bharati, Agehananda. *The Tantric Tradition*. New York: Anchor Books, 1970.

Sanskrit

Tyberg, Judith M. *The Language of the Gods*. Los Angeles, California: East-West Cultural Centre, 1976.

Tyberg, Judith M. *First Lessons in Sanskrit Reading And Grammar*. Los Angeles, California: East-West Cultural Centre. 1997

Astrology

Goswami Kriyananda. *The Wisdom and Way of Astrology*. Chicago, Illinois: The Temple Of Kriya Yoga, 2002.

Rath, Sanjay. *Vedic Remedies in Astrology*. New Delhi: Sagar Publications, 2007.

Frawley, David. *Astrology of The Seers: a Guide to Vedic/ Hindu Astrology*. Twin Lakes, Wisconsin: Lotus Press, 2000.

Cole, Freedom Tobias. *Science of Light: an Introduction to Vedic Astrology*. Nevada City, California: Freedom Cole, 2009.

Hone, Margaret E. *The Modern Text-Book of Astrology*. London: L.N. Fowler & Co. Ltd., 1969.

George, Llewellyn. *A To Z Horoscope Maker and Delineator: a Textbook of Astrology*. Saint Paul, Minnesota: Llewellyn Publications, 1976.

Tantra, Yoga of Ecstasy:
the Sadhaka's Guide to Kundalini and the Left-Hand Path

by Leigh Hurley & Phillip Hurley

Tantra is an ancient discipline with deep cosmic roots Every movement in time and space is ritual for the Tantric sadhaka, and every moment is a moment of transmutation, of alchemy. Shiva and Shakti bring us back to first principles in a feeling way that engages all of our senses, and all levels of our being. The Tantric sadhaka is enlightened by the manifestation of these first principles in their life - physically, psychologically, sociologically, and spiritually.

Tantra, Yoga of Ecstasy details ritual, practice, meditation and psychology for the serious student of Tantra.

Topics discussed include:

- ૐ Meaning and intent of classical Tantric rituals
- ૐ Tantric philosophy
- ૐ How to raise kundalini
- ૐ Shiva-Shakti meditation and Tantric initiation
- ૐ Tantra, art and creativity
- ૐ Alchemy of personal transmutation
- ૐ Deciphering the puzzle of Tantric morality
- ૐ Tantric use of astrology

www.tantrayoga.us

28863883R00091

Made in the USA
San Bernardino, CA
08 January 2016